ATLAS OF WORLD FAITHS

JUDAISM

Cath Senker

A+

Smart Apple Media

This book has been published in cooperation with
Arcturus Publishing Limited.

Series concept: Alex Woolf
Editor and picture researcher: Alex Woolf
Designer: Simon Borrough
Cartography: Encompass Graphics
Consultant: Douglas G. Heming

Picture credits:
Art Archive: 13 (Bodleian Library, Oxford).
Corbis: 5 (Fine Art Photographic Library), 7 (Alinari
Archives), 8 (Gideon Mendel), 11 (Art Archive), 14
(Bettmann), 17 (Hulton-Deutsch Collection), 19
(Hulton-Deutsch Collection), 20–21 (Les Stone/Sygma),
22 (Robert Holmes), cover and 24 (Ted Spiegel), 27
(Bettmann), 28 (Hulton-Deutsch Collection), 31
(Hulton-Deutsch Collection), 33 (H. Miller), 34
(Bettmann), 36 (David Rubinger), 38 (Ted Spiegel), 41
(Ted Spiegel).

Published in the United States by Smart Apple Media
2140 Howard Drive West, North Mankato, Minnesota
56003

Library of Congress Cataloging-in-Publication Data

Senker, Cath.
Judaism / by Cath Senker.
p. cm.—(Atlas of world faiths)
Includes index.
ISBN 978-1-59920-056-9
1. Judaism—History—Juvenile literature. 2. Jews—
History—Juvenile literature. I. Title. II. Series

BM155.3.S46 2007
296.09—dc22   2007007534

9 8 7 6 5 4 3 2 1

CONTENTS

CHAPTER 1

FROM ORIGINS TO DISPERSAL

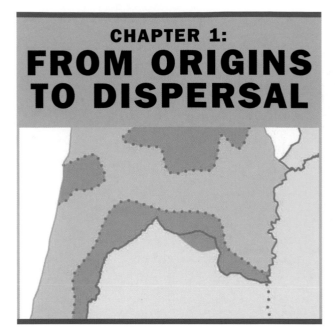

Judaism is not only a religion. The Jewish people are also an ethnic group—a people with a shared cultural background. Everyone who has a Jewish mother is considered to be Jewish. Consequently, the history of the Jewish religion is also the history of the Jewish people. Jews believe that they are descended from a tribe of people that lived in the ancient land of Canaan, which encompassed most of modern Israel, Palestine, Jordan, and Syria.

Genesis and Exodus The story of the origins of the Jews—in ancient times, also known as the Israelites or Hebrews—is found in the Torah, a sacred text containing the first five books of the Bible. According to the first book, Genesis, the original ancestor of the Jewish people was a man named

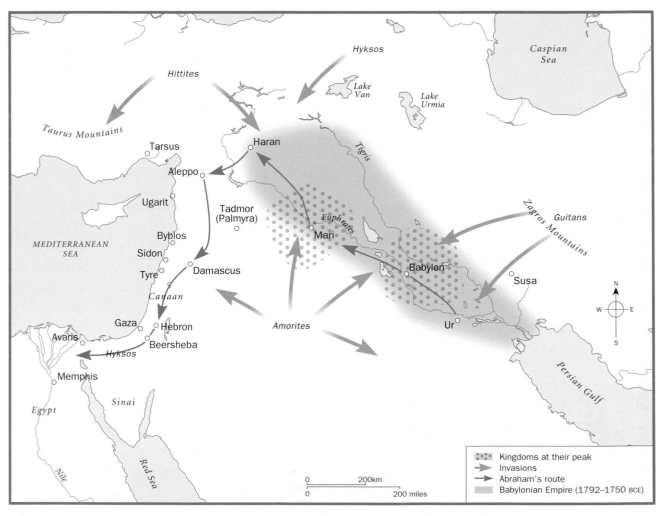

This map shows the emergence of the Jewish people from around 2000 to 1000 BCE. According to the Bible, Abraham, Isaac, and Jacob lived in the town of Beersheba, in modern-day southern Israel.

According to the account in the book of Exodus, Moses parted the waves of the sea so that the Israelites could escape from Egypt.

HEBRON, HOLY CITY

According to Genesis, Abraham's wife Sarah died in Hebron. Abraham purchased a cave and the surrounding field as a burial place for her. The tomb is also believed to be the burial place of Abraham, Isaac, Jacob, and their wives (except for Jacob's wife Rachel, who was buried near Bethlehem). The site, near the modern city of Hebron in the West Bank, is holy to Jews, Christians, and Muslims, who all see Abraham as their ancestor.

So Ephron's field in Machpelah near Mamre— both the field and the cave in it, and all the trees within the borders of the field—was legally made over to Abraham as his property in the presence of all the Hittites [a local clan] who had come to the gate of the city. Afterward, Abraham buried his wife Sarah in the cave in the field of Machpelah near Mamre (which is at Hebron) in the land of Canaan.

Genesis 23:17–19

Abraham. Around 1800 BCE, Abraham and his clan left Ur in Mesopotamia (modern-day Iraq) and moved to Canaan. Abraham had a son, Isaac, who in turn fathered Jacob. Jacob's twelve sons founded the twelve tribes of Israel. A severe famine in Canaan forced some of the tribes to settle in Egypt, where they were enslaved. Several generations later, according to the Book of Exodus, a great leader named Moses led the Israelites out of slavery to freedom in Canaan.

There is some archaeological evidence for the biblical account of Abraham's migration. Between 2000 and 1500 BCE, a nomadic group called the Amorites invaded Mesopotamia, which led to the decline of Ur. This may have prompted Abraham's departure from the region. However, scholars do not agree about the return to Canaan from Egypt. While some experts believe that the Israelites left Egypt in one exodus (mass emigration) as stated in the Bible, others believe that they settled in Canaan over a long period of time.

The mitzvoth and the Halacha

The Israelites gradually formed one nation with a set of strong religious principles. They were united by their belief in an all-powerful God who created the universe. They believed that Moses received the Torah directly from God and that the Israelites had a covenant, or special agreement, with God. God would look after them if they followed the mitzvoth (commandments) contained in the Torah. The mitzvoth set the rules of behavior for all areas of Jewish religious and daily life. For example, Jews must eat kosher food, or food that has been prepared according to Jewish law. Jews must also keep Shabbat, or the Sabbath, as a day of prayer and rest. God also gave Moses the Halacha, the oral version of the Torah, which explained how the commandments were to be kept. The Halacha was handed down from generation to generation by word of mouth.

The Torah describes how the twelve Israelite tribes in Canaan were ruled by councils of elders in peacetime. During wartime, each tribe was led by a judge, who was a tribal chieftain. There were many wars. The most powerful enemies of the Israelites were the Philistines, who had established themselves in the southern coastal plain of Canaan by the end of the eleventh century BCE. They frequently attacked the Israelite tribes. As separate tribes, the Israelites proved to be too weak to repel the Philistine threat. They eventually united into one kingdom, the kingdom of Israel.

The Israelites under the kings

The kingdom lasted from around 1000 to 586 BCE. The first king was Saul, who defeated many enemies and stopped the advance of the Philistines. Saul was succeeded by David, who crushed the Philistines and conquered the city of Jerusalem, which he made his capital. Jerusalem became the spiritual focus of the Jewish religion. David's successor, Solomon, created a powerful kingdom and brought peace and prosperity. He built fortified towns and a magnificent temple in Jerusalem.

Despite having a reputation for wisdom, Solomon sowed the seeds of division in the kingdom. For example, he taxed all of the tribes except his own tribe of Judah. After his death in 928 BCE, the northern tribes rebelled and set up their own kingdom, called Israel, while the southern tribes stayed loyal to Solomon's son and established the kingdom of Judah.

Destruction of the kingdoms

In 722 BCE, the Assyrians (a people from Mesopotamia) captured Samaria, the capital of Israel. Israel became part of the Assyrian Empire, and its population was

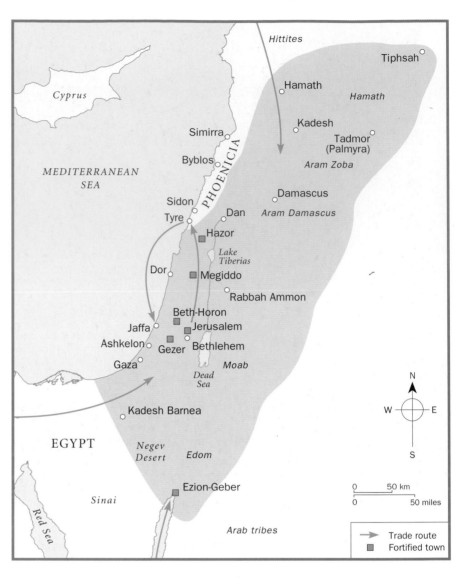

The shaded area of this map shows the area of the Kingdom of Israel under King Solomon, around 970–928 BCE. King Solomon built the fortified towns, including Megiddo, Hazor, and Gezer, to withstand sieges and protect his kingdom. Under his rule, trade with neighboring lands increased.

deported to Mesopotamia. The exiled people became known as the ten lost tribes of Israel. During the following century, the Assyrian Empire declined, and Babylon (a city in Mesopotamia) grew stronger. In 586 BCE, the Babylonians conquered Jerusalem, destroyed Solomon's temple, and ended the kingdom of Judah. The Israelites were captured or exiled to Babylon, where they formed an organized community and preserved their Jewish identity.

This description of Solomon's kingdom at its height comes from the Bible: *Judah and Israel were many, as the sand which is by the sea, in multitude, eating and drinking, and making merry. And Solomon reigned over all kingdoms from the river [Euphrates] unto the land of the Philistines, and unto the border of Egypt: they brought presents, and served Solomon all the days of his life. . . . For he had dominion over all the region on this side of the river . . . and he had peace on all sides around him. . . . And Solomon's wisdom excelled all the wisdom of all the children of the east country, and all the wisdom of Egypt . . . and his fame was in all nations.*

1 Kings 4:20–31

This is detail from a fresco (a painting created directly on a wall) by Michelangelo. The fresco is in the Sistine Chapel in Rome and depicts the prophet Ezekiel. Ezekiel was one of the Israelites exiled to Babylonia after the Babylonians conquered Jerusalem in 586. He prophesied (predicted) that the Israelites would return to their homeland.

JUDAISM

Under the Persian Empire

In 538 BCE, King Cyrus the Great of Persia (modern-day Iran) conquered Babylonia (southern Mesopotamia). He allowed all the people exiled by the Babylonians to return to their homelands, including the Jews. Most Jews chose to stay in Babylon, where they probably lived a prosperous life. Approximately 50,000 people returned to Jerusalem in several waves. They rebuilt the city, and in 516, they began reconstructing the Temple of Jerusalem that Solomon had built.

There was friction between the returning Israelites and those who had not been exiled. The returning exiles found that many Jews in Jerusalem were not following the laws of the Torah and many had married non-Jews.

Around the fifth century BCE, the religious leaders Ezra and Nehemiah reinstated Jewish law in Judah. The Jews renewed their covenant with God, vowing not to work on the Sabbath, to pay a tax to support the Temple, and to only marry other Jews.

The next major upheaval in the fortunes of the Israelites occurred when King Alexander the Great defeated the Persians in 333 BCE, and then conquered Judah the following year. King Alexander was from Macedonia in northern Greece, and he and his successors promoted Greek culture within their empire. Many Jewish people began following Hellenistic, or Greek, ways. They started to speak Greek and abandoned their Jewish traditions. Hostility developed between Hellenist and traditional Jews.

A menorah, or hanukkiyah (nine-branched candlestick), at the Western Wall in Jerusalem is lit for the festival of Hanukkah, which celebrates the restoration of the Jewish Temple in 164 BCE.

JERUSALEM

Jerusalem is holy to Jews, Christians, and Muslims. It has been the spiritual home of the Jewish people since ancient times. According to biblical accounts, Jerusalem became the capital of Israel under King David. It was once again a Jewish capital under the Hasmonaean dynasty of the Maccabees, from 164 BCE to the first century CE. During the Jewish rebellion against the Roman rule from 66 to 70 CE, Jerusalem was destroyed. The city came under Christian rule from the fourth to the seventh century and then Muslim rule for most of the period from the seventh to the twentieth century. Nevertheless, Jews around the world maintained their emotional and spiritual attachment to the holy city. In 1949, the newly formed Jewish state of Israel named Jerusalem as its capital.

The Maccabees The tensions between Greek and Jewish traditions led to a revolt in the second century BCE. At this time, the Seleucid kings, descendants of Alexander the Great's general Seleucus, dominated Judah. They tried to Hellenize Jerusalem. Between 175 and 163 BCE, the Seleucid king Antiochus IV robbed the Temple, banned the Jewish practice of circumcision, and forbade Jews from observing the Sabbath and reading the Torah. Antiochus announced that the Temple would be rededicated to the Greek god Zeus and that animals—including pigs, which were considered unclean by Jews—would be sacrificed there. Led by Judah Maccabee, the Jews rebelled. In 164 BCE, they recaptured Jerusalem and restored the Temple, an event that is celebrated at the festival of Hanukkah. Judah's family, the Hasmonaeans, established the dynasty that ruled for the following century.

This is the Kingdom of Judah around 350 BCE. Under Persian rule, from the sixth to the fourth century BCE, most of the Jewish population was concentrated around Jerusalem.

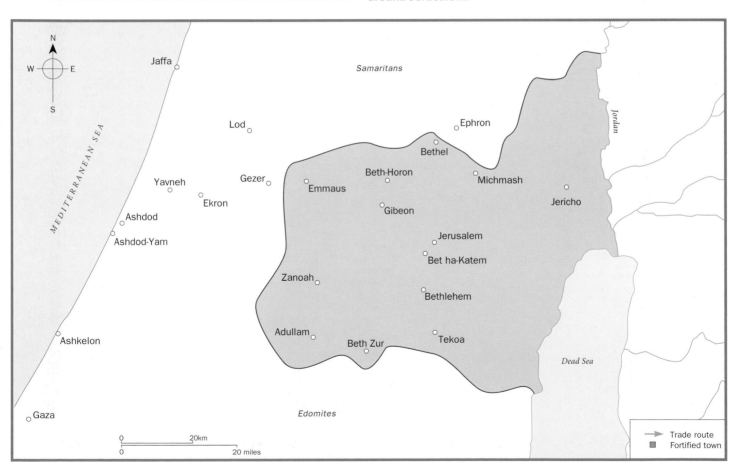

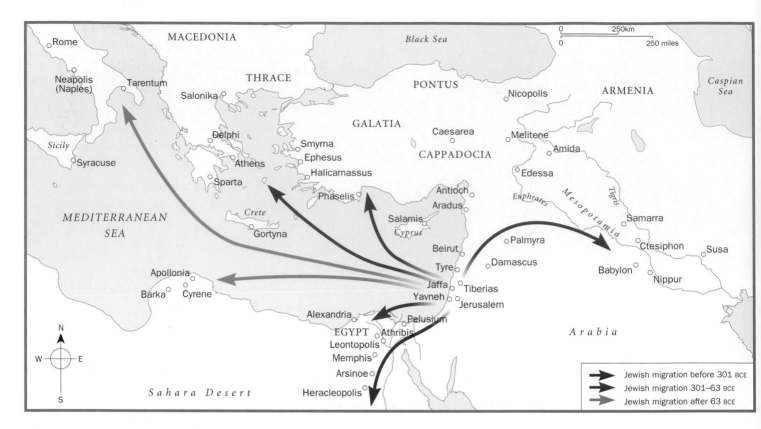

This map indicates the routes that the Jews took when they dispersed from Palestine between the fourth century BCE and the second century CE. After the destruction of the Temple in 70 CE, the area near Galilee in northern Palestine became the main Jewish center in the country, with Tiberias as the principal city.

The Romans

In 63 BCE, the Romans conquered Israel. At first, they allowed the Hasmonaeans to continue to rule in Judah. However, in 37 BCE, Herod, the Roman-appointed King of Judaea (the Roman name for Judah), attacked Jerusalem and destroyed the Hasmonaean dynasty. He executed many Jewish leaders who had been loyal to the Hasmonaeans. Although Herod rebuilt the Temple in Jerusalem, he was still hated as a cruel, foreign ruler. In 6 CE, Judaea came under direct Roman rule. Between 66 and 73 CE, Jewish rebel groups fought the Roman authorities. In 70 CE, the Romans regained control over Jerusalem and burned the Second Temple to the ground. All that remained was the Western Wall.

Led by Simon Bar Kokhba in 132 CE, a final Jewish revolt drove the Romans out of Jerusalem. But in 135, the Romans reconquered the city and enslaved its population. By this time, most of the Jews had left Judaea, which the Romans had renamed Palestine. Most of them had dispersed to different lands and formed what became known as the Diaspora, a Greek word meaning "scattering."

Judaism after the Temple

The destruction of the Temple was a disaster for the Jewish people. They had lost the central focus of their religious practice. Yet wherever Jewish people went, they maintained their traditions. After the fall of Jerusalem in 70 CE, a group of scholars living in Yavneh, in modern-day central Israel, reestablished the Sanhedrin. Formerly in Jerusalem, this was the supreme Jewish legal and religious council for Palestine and the Diaspora. The scholars began to develop a Jewish legal tradition. Scholars called rabbis interpreted the Torah and the Halacha. Many of the old Temple rituals were transferred to the synagogues (Jewish places of worship), and regular daily prayers were organized.

By the end of the second century, the interpretation of the Halacha, the oral Torah, had become increasingly complex. Much material about debates and decisions

SYNAGOGUES

The synagogue is a place where Jews meet to pray, study, and debate. The first synagogues were probably established by the Jews in exile in Babylon. Normally rectangular, synagogues are built facing toward Jerusalem. At the front is a large cupboard called an ark, where the Torah scrolls are kept. The Torah is read from a raised platform in the middle of the synagogue. Above the ark is the Ner Tamid, a lamp that burns continually to represent the burning oil lamp of the Temple and to remind worshippers of God's constant presence.

existed, but it was not arranged in an organized fashion. A rabbi named Judah Ha-Nasi (ca. 135–220) began compiling oral Jewish law so that the Jews would have a legal code to live by. The result was the Mishna, a collection of Jewish laws covering a range of human activities, including farming, taxes, festivals, marriage, crime, and ritual purity. In the fourth century CE, rabbis in Palestine put together the Palestinian Talmud. It contained the Mishna and a record of scholarly discussions about Jewish law, customs, and ethics. Similar work was undertaken by rabbis in Babylon, who created the Babylonian Talmud around 500 CE. According to Jewish law, authority lies with the most recent work, and so Jews came to regard the Babylonian Talmud as the main source for their laws.

A painting of the destruction of the Second Temple in Jerusalem by Roman soldiers in 70 CE by the nineteenth-century Italian painter, Francesco Hayez. The Temple was never rebuilt and all that remains is the Western, or Wailing, Wall.

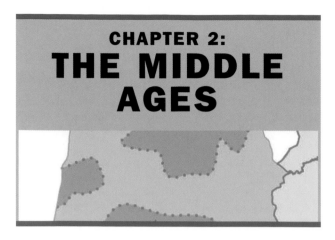

CHAPTER 2: THE MIDDLE AGES

In the fourth century, Christianity became the official religion of the Roman Empire, which controlled Europe, the Middle East, and North Africa. Life grew difficult for the Jews living under Christian rule. The Christian church was not tolerant of Judaism. Christians believed that God had rejected the Jews and had delivered a new message to humanity through Jesus Christ.

Jesus Christ, or Jesus of Nazareth, was a teacher and healer in Palestine around 28–30 CE. Encouraged by the leaders of the Jewish community, Jesus was put to death by the Roman authorities, who feared that Jesus's growing popularity could undermine their power.

Christians believed Jesus to be the son of God. They said that the Jews had failed to heed the new message and were responsible for Jesus's death. Roman law made it illegal to convert to Judaism and for a Christian and a Jew to marry. At the beginning of the fifth century, Jews were not allowed to hold government positions. During the Middle Ages (500–1500), the Christian church dominated most aspects of life in Europe, and Jews who lived there often experienced hatred and humiliation. Life was generally easier for Jews living under Islamic rule in the Middle East, North Africa, and Spain.

Jews under Islam
In the early seventh century, the religion of Islam arose under the leadership of its founder, the Prophet Muhammad. The followers

This illustration of Jonah being swallowed by a large fish is from the 1299 Cervera Bible. There was a thriving Jewish community in Cervera, a small town in Catalonia, Spain.

of Islam were called Muslims, and Islam spread rapidly from its base in the Arabian Peninsula. By 744, Syria, Palestine, Egypt, Persia (modern-day Iran), and Mesopotamia (modern-day Iraq) had embraced the new faith. The rulers of this new Islamic empire saw Christians and Jews as fellow worshippers of the one true God and allowed them to practice their faiths. However, Jews were restricted in certain ways. For example, they had to wear special clothing, and as non-Muslims, they had to pay an annual tax. Yet Jews prospered under Islamic rule, becoming skilled craftsmen and taking advantage of the empire's established trade networks to become successful merchants and traders.

The Jewish people governed their own communities, and they established religious academies called yeshivas. The gaon, the head of the yeshiva, was the senior religious authority in the community. He organized the Jewish courts and appointed all of the religious officials, including the ritual butchers, who made sure animals were killed for food according to the Jewish dietary laws.

Although Jewish people maintained their separate identity, their culture was influenced by Islamic traditions, and Jewish scholars wrote philosophical

KARAISM

Karaism was an anti-rabbinic sect, or group opposed to rabbis, that emerged in the ninth century. The Karaites based their beliefs on the ideas of Anan ben David, a Persian Jew who had lived during the eighth century. Ben David's principle was "search thoroughly in the Torah and do not rely on my opinion." He claimed that all of the Jewish law was contained in the Torah and that the rabbis' spoken interpretations were unnecessary. In the ninth century, Benjamin ben Moses Nahawendi was the first to use the term "Karaite." He established a Karaite sect in Iran, and the doctrine spread. By the eleventh century, there were Karaites throughout the Muslim world and the Byzantine Empire (the Christian Eastern Roman Empire). The movement declined by the late sixteenth century.

and scientific works in Arabic. In North Africa and Al-Andalus (the large part of Spain under Muslim rule), Jewish culture blossomed during the tenth and eleventh centuries.

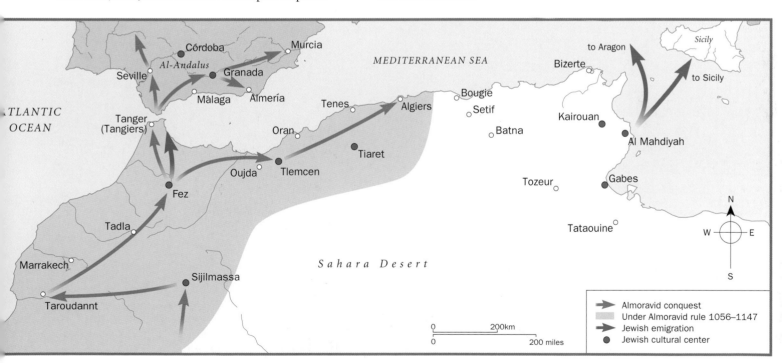

This map of North Africa and Al-Andalus (present-day Andalusia) in the tenth and eleventh centuries shows the Jewish cultural centers and the conquests by the Muslim Almoravid dynasty.

North African Jewish scholars wrote important commentaries on the Talmud. Some, including the Tunisian Isaac ben Solomon Israeli, wrote on secular (nonreligious) subjects such as medicine and philosophy. There were also several important Jewish statesmen and philosophers. Hasdai ibn Shaprut (ca. 915–ca. 975), from the city of Córdoba in Al-Andalus, was head of the Jewish community, court physician to the Muslim leaders, and a diplomat who helped his leaders negotiate with the Christians in northern Spain. The poet and philosopher Solomon ibn Gabirol

KABBALA

Kabbala, meaning "that which is received," is a study of the secrets contained within the Torah; there were hints of mystical speculation in the Talmud. For example, in a rabbinic commentary on the Book of Genesis, the custom was to recite the secret traditions in a whisper so that only educated people could know the "secrets" of the Torah. In the twelfth century, mystical speculation led to the development of the Kabbala tradition in southern France. One significant work was the late-twelfth-century *Sefer ha-Bahir* (Book of Brightness) that explains how God created the universe and describes the mystical significance of the shapes and sounds of the Hebrew alphabet— Hebrew is the sacred language of the Jews. In the thirteenth century, a school of Kabbala developed in Girona, in northern Spain. Rabbi Moses de Leon (1250–1305) drew on the teachings of the Girona school to produce the influential *Sefer ha-Zohar* (The Book of Splendor). This work explains the inner, mystical meaning of the Torah and teaches that human action in the service of God can help repair disharmony in the world and bring union with God. After the Jews were expelled from Spain in 1492, some made their way to Safed in northern Palestine. Safed became the principal center of the development of the Kabbala in the sixteenth century.

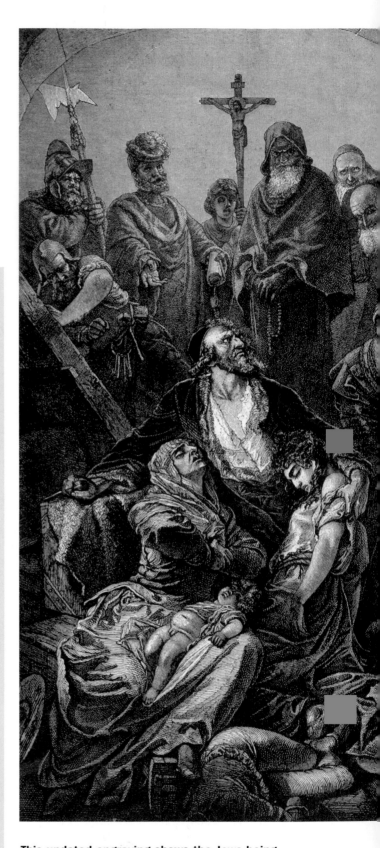

This undated engraving shows the Jews being expelled from Spain in 1492 by order of the Inquisition. Only Jews who had converted to Christianity were allowed to remain.

(ca. 1022–ca. 1070) wrote poetry modeled on the Arabic style of the time, but with biblical influences from his Jewish education.

Persecution

In 1146, the Muslim Almohad dynasty from North Africa began to conquer Al-Andalus. The Almohads did not allow Jews to follow their religion, closing their yeshivas and synagogues and forcing them to convert to Islam. Many Jews fled north to the Christian-ruled part of Spain, where Jews were accepted, while others practiced their faith in secret. Some escaped to North Africa, including the philosopher Maimonides (1135–1204). Despite the difficulties, this was a period of enormous Jewish creativity. Maimonides produced an important code of Jewish law, the Mishneh Torah, while the Jewish mystical work, *Sefer ha-Zohar*, was compiled by Rabbi Moses de Leon (1250–1305).

Reconquest

During the twelfth century, Christian forces reconquered much of Al-Andalus. At first, Jews fared well under Christian rule, but in the late fourteenth century they began to be persecuted. Many were forced to convert to Christianity, but the conversos—or converts—were increasingly regarded with suspicion. In around 1480, the Spanish Inquisition began. The Spanish Inquisition was a court set up by Spain's Christian rulers to try suspected heretics—people whose beliefs contradict established Christian teaching. Thousands of people were convicted of heresy. Their property was confiscated, or in many cases, they were burned to death at the stake. In 1492, the Jews were driven out of Spain altogether, and they became scattered around North Africa, Italy, the Netherlands, and the Ottoman Empire (an Islamic empire covering much of southeastern Europe, the Middle East, and North Africa).

In January 1492, following the fall of Granada, the Christian reconquest of Spain was complete. King Ferdinand and Queen Isabella of Spain ordered all Jews to leave the country.

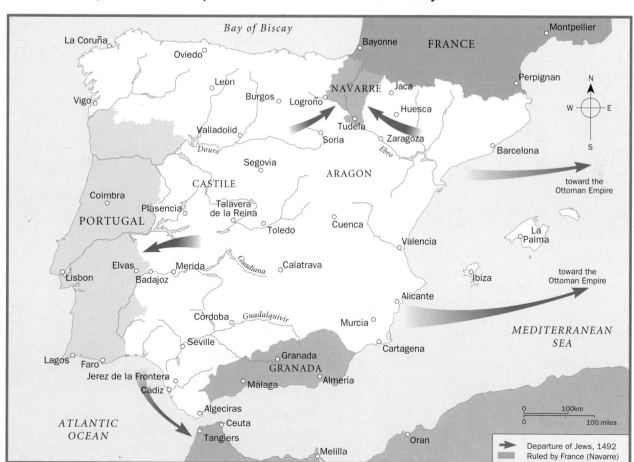

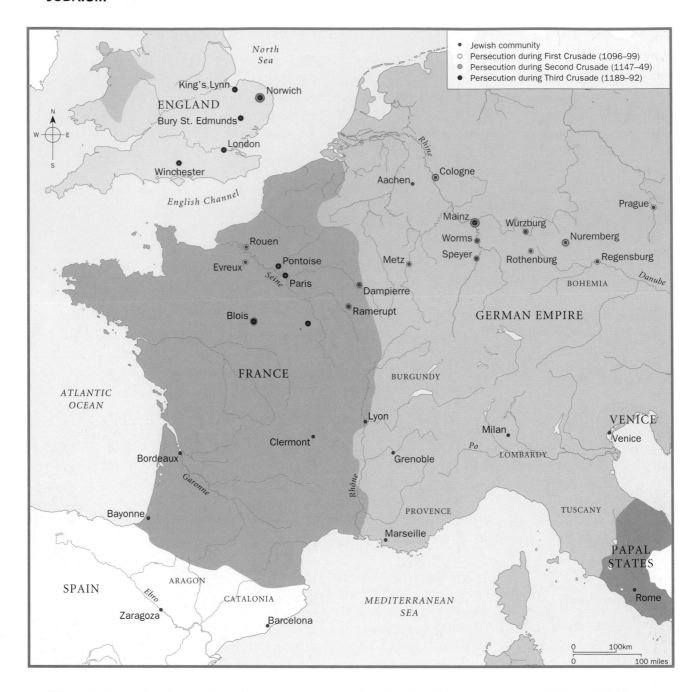

This map shows the places where Jews were persecuted during the Crusades, between 1096 and 1348.

Map legend:
- Jewish community
- Persecution during First Crusade (1096–99)
- Persecution during Second Crusade (1147–49)
- Persecution during Third Crusade (1189–92)

Jews in Christian Europe

Under Christian rule, Jews in central and western European countries endured mistrust that regularly turned to violent attacks. In 1096, the Crusades began as a struggle by western European Christian forces to regain the Holy Land, including Jerusalem, from the Muslims. The intensified religious fervor led to a rise in attacks on Jewish communities. For instance, Jews were killed in several towns in the Rhineland area of Germany.

During this time, Jews were accused of various crimes. In 1144, the Jews of Norwich, England, were charged with using the blood of Christian children to make matzo (bread made without yeast) for the Jewish festival of Passover. This false accusation, known as "blood libel," spread all over Europe.

Jews were hated not only for religious reasons, but also because of their reputation as moneylenders. Jews were excluded from numerous professions and trades, so many had turned to moneylending, a job forbidden to Christians because they were not allowed to charge interest on loans. Moneylenders were unpopular among the poor, who relied on their services yet resented being in debt to them.

Around Europe, laws were introduced that made life harder for the Jews. For instance, in 1215 a Roman Catholic council forced all Jews in Europe to wear a badge or hat to identify themselves as Jewish. During the fourteenth and fifteenth centuries, the practice of segregating Jews spread around Europe. In many places, Jews were forced to live in a poor part of the town called a ghetto. The Jews were locked in at night and watched by guards.

At times, some rulers simply decided to expel their Jewish populations completely. In 1290, Jews were banished from England. Several times during the fourteenth century, Jews in France were expelled, then allowed to return before finally being forced out in 1394. When the Black Death, or plague, raged through Europe in the mid-fourteenth century, Jews were widely blamed for causing the fatal disease and many were murdered by angry mobs. In the fifteenth and sixteenth centuries, Jews were regularly expelled by German cities and forced to move to other cities that would accept them. Poland remained an exception, and beginning in the thirteenth century, Jews were protected there.

This anti-Semitic illustration, from around 1478, depicts the common medieval belief that Jewish people used the blood of Christian children in their religious rituals.

PASSOVER

The Jewish people have kept their history and their sense of community alive through their customs. Every year, they celebrate the festival of Passover to remember their ancestors' escape from slavery in Egypt. Families gather for a seder —a ritual meal—on the first evening of the eight-day festival. They retell the story of the Exodus and carry out rituals that help them feel connected to their ancestors. They eat matzo, the unleavened bread that the Israelites had to eat on their journey out of Egypt. The book read at the seder is called the Haggadah. Since the Middle Ages, the Haggadah has ended with the phrase "Next year in Jerusalem," to express the Jewish yearning for their holy land and the long-lost Temple of Jerusalem.

CHAPTER 3: JEWS AROUND THE WORLD

MATTEO RICCI AND THE KAIFENG JEWS

The Italian priest Matteo Ricci (1552–1610) recounted in his letters how he discovered the Jews of China through a fascinating encounter. In 1605, a Kaifeng Jew named Ai Tien was called to a meeting with Ricci at his home in Beijing. Ai Tien had heard that, unlike the Chinese, the foreign traveler Ricci believed in one God. Ai Tien thought that Ricci must be a Jewish rabbi, while Ricci believed Ai Tien to be a Christian. The pair looked at a painting together. Ai Tien thought it showed four of the twelve sons of Jacob and was surprised to learn they were the four Apostles of Christ. Ai Tien wondered who Christ was. Ricci then realized that Ai Tien was in fact Jewish, not Christian, and he told him about Christianity.

Beginning in the second century, Jews were widely dispersed to many countries, including Persia, Yemen, China, and India, where Jewish communities remained until the twentieth century. Following the expulsions from European countries during the Middle Ages, the major centers of Judaism were the Ottoman Empire (in the Middle East and North Africa) and Poland, where two distinct Jewish cultures developed: the Ottoman Sephardi and the European Ashkenazi.

Persia Although the Jews were permitted to return to Israel when Persia conquered Babylonia in 538 BCE, many remained in Babylon and spread throughout the towns of Babylonia and Persia. In the mid-seventh

The Jewish world in 1200: the Jews were widely dispersed by this time.

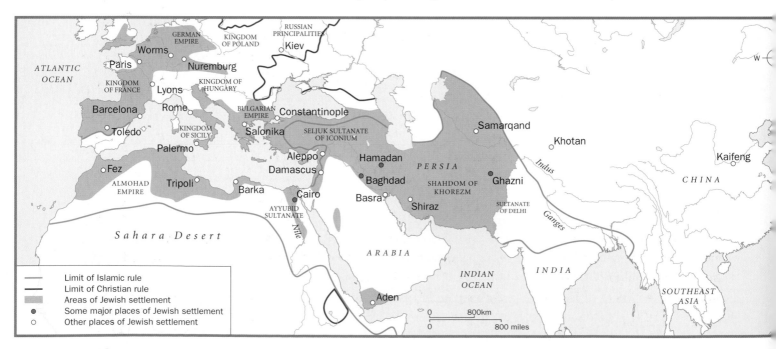

- Limit of Islamic rule
- Limit of Christian rule
- Areas of Jewish settlement
- ● Some major places of Jewish settlement
- ○ Other places of Jewish settlement

These Yemeni Jews, studying a map of Israel, were brought to Israel by the Israeli government in 1949–50. Because their rights as Jews were restricted, most Yemeni Jews decided to emigrate to Israel. Very few Jews remain in Yemen today.

century, the Arab Muslims conquered Persia. They allowed the Jews to practice their religion and to engage in any occupation. However, under the Safavid (1502–1736) and Qajar dynasties (1794–1925), the Jews were forced to convert to Islam or they were killed. Their position improved after that, but in 1979, a radical Islamic government took power in Iran, leading to an exodus of Iranian Jews.

Yemen Jews probably arrived in Yemen between the third century BCE and the third century CE, although the first evidence of their presence dates from the sixth century CE. Like Jews in other Muslim lands, the Yemeni Jews were allowed to follow their faith. In the late nineteenth century, Yemeni Jews began to emigrate to Palestine. In 1949 and 1950, most of the remaining Jews in Yemen were brought to the newly established state of Israel (founded in 1948).

China There is evidence of a Jewish presence in China from the eighth century, although Jews may have arrived centuries earlier. Kaifeng, in eastern China, had a Jewish community dating from the eleventh century, and in 1163, a synagogue was built there. Through the years, the Kaifeng Jews either dispersed or they assimilated—mingled with the majority Chinese and lost their Jewish identity.

Modern Jewish communities formed again during the nineteenth and twentieth centuries. The greatest number of Jews came as refugees during World War II (1939–45), but most dispersed to different countries after the war.

India The largest group of Indian Jews, the Bene Israel, claimed to have migrated to India from Palestine in the second century BCE, although there is no actual evidence of this. It is more likely that Jewish people came to India from Spain, Portugal, Persia, Afghanistan, and Mesopotamia (modern-day Iraq) during the sixteenth and seventeenth centuries.

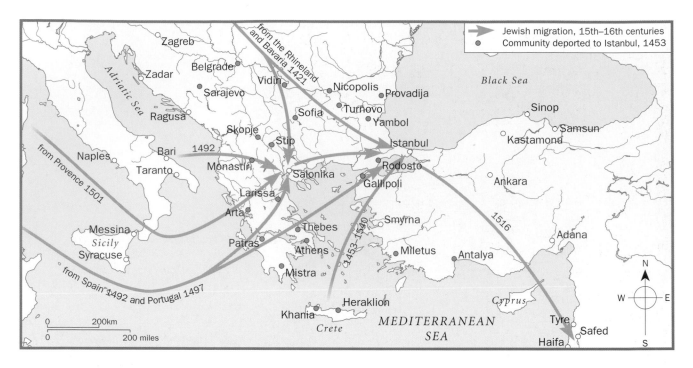

This map shows the main migrations of Jewish communities to the Ottoman Empire in the fifteenth and sixteenth centuries. At the end of the fifteenth century, around 20,000 Jews—who had been expelled from Spain—went to Salonika (present-day Thessaloniki, Greece).

Although they followed a similar lifestyle in many ways to their Hindu and Muslim neighbors, the Bene Israel also practiced Jewish customs, such as circumcision and observing the Sabbath and kosher food laws. The Jewish communities maintained their independence when India was under British rule (1858–1947), but most moved to Israel after its establishment in 1948.

Ethiopia

Jewish Ethiopians call themselves Beta Esrael and are also known as Falashas. According to their traditions, they came to Ethiopia after the exodus from Egypt or after the destruction of the First Temple. Little is known about their history before the thirteenth century. Between the thirteenth and fifteenth centuries, the Beta Esrael struggled against Muslim and Christian rulers to retain their independence. They continued to survive on the margins of Ethiopian society until the twentieth century. Israel did not accept them as Jews at first, and they were not formally recognized as Jews until 1973. Most Beta Esrael were brought to Israel in two extraordinary rescue operations: first during a famine in 1984 and then during political unrest in 1991.

Sephardim and Ashkenazim

Although Jews were spread around the world, in the Middle Ages, the majority were concentrated in Spain and the Islamic countries and also in northern and eastern Europe. The Jews who were expelled from Spain in 1492 and from Portugal in 1497 mainly migrated to the Muslim Ottoman Empire in North Africa and the Middle East. They became known as the Sephardim (from the Hebrew word for Spain). Jews were permitted to follow their faith in the Ottoman Empire as long as they accepted Muslim rule and paid the tax for non-Muslims. A distinctive Sephardi culture developed. Jews spoke their own language, called Ladino, which included Spanish and Hebrew words. The Sephardic Jews prospered under Ottoman rule. They set up the empire's first printing press in 1493, and Jewish literature flourished. Most court physicians were Jews, as were many diplomats.

The Jews who were forced out of Germany in the fifteenth and sixteenth centuries settled in Poland. They became known as Ashkenazim (from the Hebrew word for Germany). They spoke their own dialect, Yiddish, which contained elements of German and Hebrew, and they played eastern European music. Most Jews lived in their own shtetls (villages) with synagogues and yeshivas.

SEPHARDI AND ASHKENAZI PRACTICES

Sephardi and Ashkenazi Jews all use Hebrew as their language of worship, read the same Torah and Talmud, say the same prayers, eat kosher food, and celebrate the same festivals. However, they have separate synagogues because they have different traditions of worship. For example, Sephardis use their own poems and psalms (sacred songs) in their services. They chant the Torah in a different way from Ashkenazis and sing prayers to different melodies.

In the Palestinian town of Safed in the mid-1500s, Sephardi rabbi Joseph Karo compiled a legal code for Sephardi Judaism called the *Shulchan Arukh*, which was published in 1565. Around 1570, it was reissued with modifications by Rabbi Moses Isserles to include Ashkenazi customs so that guidance for the religious behavior of both Sephardi and Ashkenazi communities would be contained in a single book. Nevertheless, the two traditions maintained their separate practices.

Ethiopian Jews gather outside the Israeli Embassy in the Ethiopian capital Addis Ababa in 1991. They were airlifted to Israel during Operation Solomon.

Poland and Lithuania became centers of Jewish cultural life. For example, the Yeshybot yeshiva was established in Lublin, Poland, in 1515 and became an important place for Talmudic study. Rabbi Moses Isserles, who helped write the *Shulchan Arukh*, studied there, and the city became known as the "Jewish Oxford" (after Oxford University in England). Because of their emphasis on religious study, the Jewish people had a higher literacy rate than their Christian neighbors. Although they suffered some discrimination, such as having to wear distinctive clothing, Jews were allowed to run their own communities. Many worked for the nobility (the wealthy landowners), running their estates and collecting taxes from the peasantry.

However, anti-Jewish hatred grew in Poland during the seventeenth century. In 1648, the Cossacks, a Ukrainian people living under Polish authority, rebelled against the Polish nobility. Led by Bohdan Khmelnytsky, they punished the Jews because they worked for the nobility. During this period, it is estimated that a quarter of the Jewish community in Poland was either tortured or massacred, while others were sold into slavery. The Jews were also attacked by the Russians, who were allied with Khmelnytsky. When the Swedes invaded western Poland, Jewish people were assaulted by Poles who believed that the Jews had encouraged the invasion. The Cossacks committed further violence against the Jews in the eighteenth century. By 1795, Poland was divided and the Jewish population was split among Russia, Prussia, and Austria.

Religious movements

Life was clearly difficult for Polish Jews in the eighteenth century. During these hard times, a new religious movement arose, founded by Rabbi Israel ben Eliezer (1698–1760), also known as the Ba'al Shem Tov (Master of the Good Name), or the Besht. The movement was based on a spirited, joyful worship of God under the guidance of a zaddik (spiritual leader). The followers of the Besht were known as the Hasidim (Pious Ones), and after ben Eliezer's death in 1760, the Hasidic movement spread throughout Poland and eastern Europe.

However, when the Hasidic movement reached Lithuania in the late eighteenth century, it was strongly

THE BA'AL SHEM TOV

The Ba'al Shem Tov did not write down his teachings, but his sayings were recorded by his disciples. In this saying, he expresses his belief in *devekut* (devotion to God): *Every single thing one sees or hears is an instruction for his conduct in the service of God. This is the idea of spiritual service— to comprehend and discern in all things a way in which to serve God.*

Hasidic Jews in modern-day Jaffa, Israel, in their typical clothing. The movement spread to the United States in the late nineteenth century, and the majority of hasidim currently live in the U.S.

resisted. Rabbi Elijah ben Solomon Zalman (1720–97), the gaon of the city of Vilna, established a movement in opposition to the Hasidim, which the Hasidim described as the Mitnaggedim (Opponents). The Mitnaggedim defended traditional values, including the intensive study of the Torah and Talmud, and rejected the honoring of zaddikim (spiritual leaders). Both movements ran yeshivas that taught their particular doctrines. The conflict subsided in the nineteenth century, when the groups united to oppose the Haskalah (see pages 24–25).

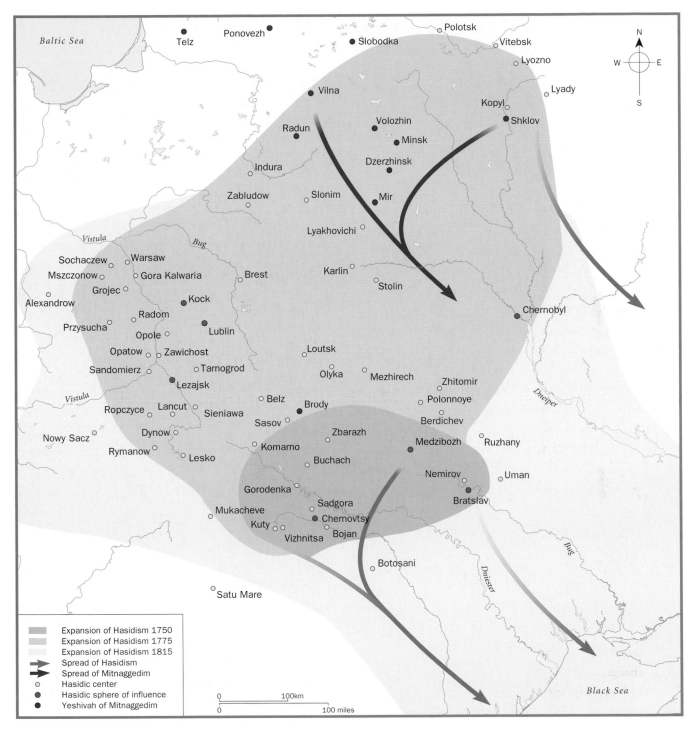

This map shows the expansion of the Hasidic movement in the eighteenth and nineteenth centuries, as well as the influence of the Mitnaggedim, who opposed Hasidism. At this time, Lublin, Vilna, and Mukacheve were all important Jewish cultural centers.

CHAPTER 4:
ENLIGHTENMENT TO WORLD WAR

In the late seventeenth century, western European countries began to allow Jews to return. For example, in 1670, the ruler of Brandenburg, Germany, invited Jews to settle there because they were good traders and could help revive the economy after the Thirty Years' War (1618–48). Around the same time, Jews were permitted to return to France. Yet Jews were still barred from many occupations. For example, they were not allowed to join craft and trade guilds (associations formed to give help and protection to their members). In England, Jews could neither hold public office nor attend college. However, toward the end of the eighteenth century, some of the restrictions were lifted in central Europe. In France, Jews were given full civil rights after the French Revolution of 1789. During the nineteenth century, equal rights were extended to all Jewish people in Europe, except those living in the Russian Empire.

Movements in Judaism There were also changes within the Jewish community during this period. Jewish scholars were influenced by the Enlightenment, an eighteenth-century movement in western Europe that emphasized reason and science in the study of the human and natural world. The Jewish Enlightenment, known as the Haskalah, took place in

At this Yom Kippur service in a Reform synagogue, there is no separation between men and women.

western Europe in the late eighteenth and early nineteenth centuries. Jewish thinkers applied the principles of the Enlightenment to their religion. The most influential thinker, Moses Mendelssohn (1729–86) of Berlin, Germany, believed that Jews should try to fit in better with the society around them. They should study secular (nonreligious) as well as religious subjects and learn the language of their adopted country. His followers were known as the *maskilim*. They laid the foundations for the Reform Movement.

Israel Jacobson (1768–1828) began the Reform Movement in Germany. He set up schools where Jewish children learned secular as well as religious subjects. The movement attempted to adapt Judaism to the conditions of the modern world and make it easier for Jews to be full citizens of their country. Reform synagogue services were in German rather than Hebrew, and men and women—traditionally seated apart—sat together. Work was permitted on the Sabbath, and people no longer had to follow the kosher food laws.

Many Jews feared that these changes would lead to assimilation. A division grew between Reform and traditional, or Orthodox, Jews. In Germany, the most prominent Orthodox thinker was Samson Raphael Hirsch (1808–88). Hirsch believed that Jews should follow traditional practices, but he accepted that they could also have a secular education. This type of thinking became known as Neo-Orthodoxy, or new Orthodoxy.

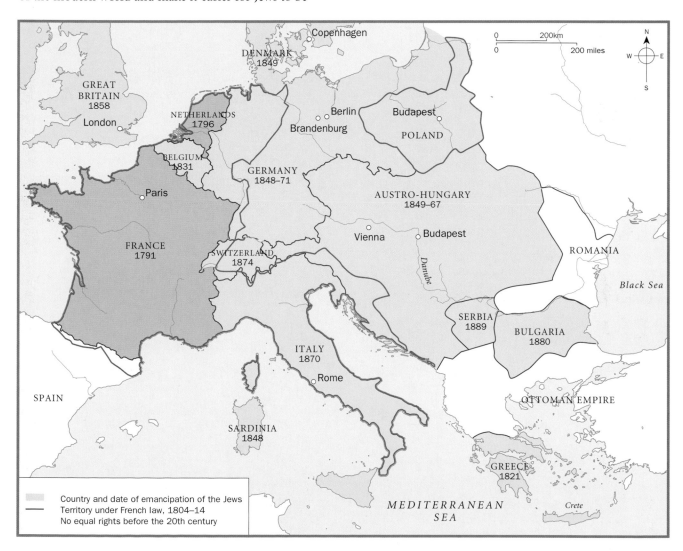

This map shows the European countries that emancipated the Jews—freeing them from legal, social, and political restrictions—along with the date of their emancipation.

Some Orthodox Jews opposed all changes to Judaism. In Germany, Rabbi Moses Sofer challenged the Reform Movement in the early 1800s. His motto was: "Anything new is forbidden by the Torah." His views influenced the development of Haredi Judaism (see page 39).

Anti-Semitism

In the late nineteenth century, many European states experienced a growing sense of nationalism. Individual nations wanted to develop their own national identity, based on the dominant ethnic group in society. Minority groups with their own customs, especially the Jews, were seen as outsiders that posed a threat to social unity. The increasing presence of Jews in mainstream society—in professions, finance, and the arts—was resented, as was their growing wealth and economic power. A modern form of anti-Semitism (hostility to Jews) emerged, based on so-called "racial," rather than religious, differences. Many believed that the Jews were a sinister race that wanted to dominate the world.

In this excerpt from Theodor Herzl's 1896 book *The Jewish State*, he outlines his view of anti-Semitism: *The Jewish question exists wherever Jews live in perceptible numbers. Where it does not exist, it is carried by Jews in the course of their migrations. We naturally move to those places where we are not persecuted, and there our presence produces persecution. This is the case in every country, and will remain so, even in those highly civilized—for instance, France—until the Jewish question finds a solution on a political basis. The unfortunate Jews are now carrying the seeds of anti-Semitism into England; they have already introduced it into America.*

Anti-Semitism became widespread in Germany and France and was adopted as official state policy in Russia. In 1880s Russia, new restrictions were placed

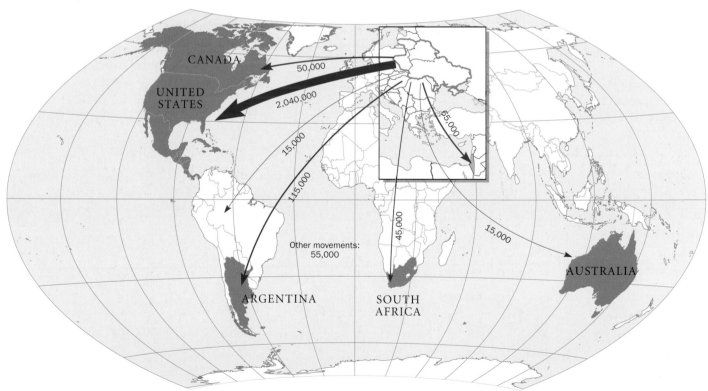

This map shows the numbers of Jews that emigrated from eastern Europe between 1881 and 1914 and the countries they moved to.

This illustration portrays an assault on Jews in Kiev in the Russian Empire during the 1880s. The police look on and do nothing to stop the violence.

on where Jews could settle, and strict quotas were imposed to limit the number of Jews in professions and colleges. Anti-Semitic works were published. The best known was the *Protocols of the Elders of Zion*, first published in Russia in 1903. Apparently written by a secret Jewish organization determined to achieve world domination, it was in fact a fraud intended to stir anti-Semitism. In Russia and other parts of eastern Europe, there were waves of pogroms between 1881 and 1921—outbreaks of violence against Jewish communities, including murder, rape, and the destruction of property.

Zionism Jewish people reacted in various ways to the devastating attacks. A minority was drawn to the Zionist movement, founded by an Austro-Hungarian

Jewish journalist, Theodor Herzl. Herzl came to believe that anti-Semitism would always exist, and the only solution was to establish a state for the Jews in the historic land of Israel. In 1897, he founded the World Zionist Organization. There were few Jews living in Palestine at the time, but the pogroms in eastern Europe led to increased Jewish emigration there.

Migration The majority of Jews who emigrated from Europe to escape persecution went to the U.S. rather than Palestine. In 1880, there were about 250,000 Jews in the U.S., mostly of German origin. Between 1881 and 1914, about two million eastern European Jews moved to the U.S.; others moved to western Europe, South Africa, Argentina (in South America), and Canada.

Most of the Jewish immigrants arriving in their host countries were deeply religious and very poor. By contrast, existing Jewish communities in these countries tended to be well assimilated. Immigrants often found it hard to adjust to their new situation. In the United Kingdom, for example, non-Jewish employers expected Jews to work on the Sabbath. However, within a couple of generations, the immigrants had adapted to life in their adopted countries.

Socialism Some Jewish people reacted to anti-Semitism by joining revolutionary socialist movements. As a persecuted people, Jews were attracted to the socialist thinkers' radical idea of an equal society. Rather than emigrating or establishing a Jewish state, socialist Jews believed they should struggle alongside other workers to overthrow existing governments. In 1897, Jewish workers established the Bund—the General Jewish Workers' Union of Lithuania, Poland, and Russia. Jewish people, such as Leon Trotsky, played a prominent role in the 1917 revolution in Russia, while a Jewish woman, Rosa Luxemburg, was one of the leaders of the 1918–19 uprising in Germany.

The revolutionary socialist government in Russia overturned the laws against Jews but was also committed to the abolition of religion. There was a campaign against religious practices. Many Jewish organizations were closed down in 1918, and it was against the law to teach Hebrew. The government also closed the small businesses on which many Jews relied for a living and forced Jewish people into jobs in agriculture and heavy industry.

World War I In 1914, war broke out among the major European powers. World

A photograph of German-Jewish revolutionary Rosa Luxemburg in about 1914. In 1918, her organization, the Communist Party of Germany, attempted to lead a revolution. It failed, and she was murdered in January 1919 by right-wing opponents.

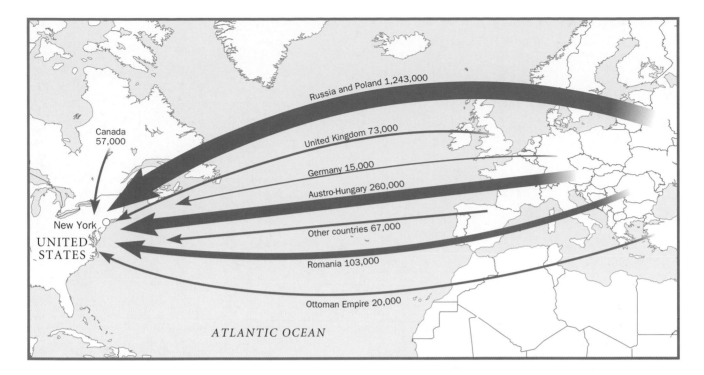

Russia and Poland 1,243,000

Canada 57,000

United Kingdom 73,000

Germany 15,000

Austro-Hungary 260,000

New York

UNITED STATES

Other countries 67,000

Romania 103,000

Ottoman Empire 20,000

ATLANTIC OCEAN

The U.S. was the most popular destination for Jewish emigrants from all eastern European countries. This map shows the numbers that left between 1899 and 1914.

War I brought anti-Semitic feelings into sharp focus. At this time, around four million Jews were living on the war's eastern front, where Russia was fighting Germany and Austria-Hungary. The Russian government suspected that Jews were collaborating with the enemy and deported them from the region. This action severely tested Jewish loyalty to Russia. Nevertheless, around half a million Jews joined the Russian army.

In other lands, large numbers of Jews also fought for their country—nearly 100,000 in Germany. Yet hostility toward Jews continued. They were accused of avoiding army service and of profiteering—making an unreasonable profit from selling goods during the war. In the U.S. and the UK, Jews were suspected of supporting Germany, the enemy, because of their hostility toward Russia. Jews of German origin were forced to sign a declaration of loyalty to their host country.

After the war ended in 1918, German Jews were blamed for their country's defeat, while in Russia opponents of the 1917 Revolution blamed Jews for the Revolution's success.

WELFARE ORGANIZATIONS IN THE U.S.

Throughout history, Jews used their own resources to provide welfare for the less fortunate in their community. It was an obligation within Jewish law to help the needy by putting donations in the *kuppah*, or collection box. The funds were distributed to good causes, ranging from soup kitchens to burial societies that provided funerals for the poorest people.

When penniless eastern European Jews arrived in the U.S., this system continued. In 1895, the Jews of Boston set up the first centralized Jewish organization, which brought together all of the local welfare groups. The model spread to other American cities. As well as providing health care and housing for the elderly, the federations opened Jewish community centers that offered cultural, educational, and recreational activities.

CHAPTER 5: THE HOLOCAUST AND ISRAEL

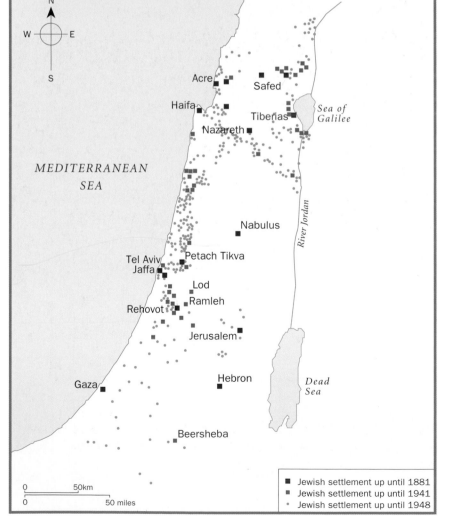

The persecution of Jews in eastern European countries continued after World War I. Despite the fact that many Jews had fought and given their lives for their country during the war, they continued to be viewed by many as outsiders who did not have their nation's interests at heart. To avoid persecution, Jews continued to leave in large numbers for the U.S., western Europe, and elsewhere. Yet, between 1921 and 1924, the U.S. and other Western countries restricted Jewish immigration. Anti-Semitism existed in these nations, too.

Against this background, support for Zionism grew. In 1918, the British captured Palestine from the collapsing Ottoman Empire, and two years later, the UK established a mandate (rule) over the country. In the Balfour Declaration of 1917, the UK had expressed support for the establishment of a Jewish homeland in Palestine. This declaration encouraged the Zionists, and Jewish emigration to Palestine increased. The Jewish community grew from 90,000 at the end of World War I, to about 160,000 in 1929, to nearly 500,000 by 1939.

The Palestinian community resisted the influx of settlers. In 1921, the Jewish National Fund purchased Palestinian land for Jewish settlement, evicting many Palestinians from their homes. This led to anti-Zionist riots. Several Arab organizations protested to the British about Jewish immigration; there were further riots in 1929 and a widespread rebellion between 1936 and 1939. It proved impossible to reconcile the interests of the Zionists and the Palestinians.

This map indicates the growth of Jewish settlements in Palestine from the late nineteenth century until the establishment of the state of Israel in 1948.

The rise of Nazism

In the early 1930s, a severe economic depression hit the U.S. and Europe. Germany was badly affected. Between 1930 and 1933, over six million German people were out of work. The government was in crisis and needed a strong leader. In 1933, the leader of the Nationalist Socialist German Workers' (Nazi) party, Adolf Hitler, was appointed chancellor of Germany. Hitler blamed the Jews and Communists for Germany's economic problems. He believed that the Germans were a "master" race and that Germany could be restored to greatness by armed conquest of neighboring lands.

Between 1933 and 1939, Hitler introduced a series of anti-Jewish laws. German Jews were deprived of citizenship, lost their professional jobs, and soon lost all their freedoms. In 1938, during an organized Nazi attack that became known as Kristallnacht (Night of Broken Glass), hundreds of synagogues in Germany and Austria were burned, thousands of Jewish businesses were destroyed, and at least 35 Jews were murdered.

A man clears up the broken glass in a Jewish-owned bed store after it was damaged the previous night during Kristallnacht, November 1938. The Nazis had ordered the police and fire services not to interfere with the attacks unless non-Jewish property was threatened with damage.

KRISTALLNACHT

Ernest Günter Fontheim recalled his experience of Kristallnacht as a schoolboy in Berlin: *The air was filled with the acrid smell of smoke. I was wedged in the middle of a hostile crowd, which was in an ugly mood shouting anti-Semitic slogans. I was completely hypnotized by the burning synagogue and was totally oblivious to any possible danger. I thought of the many times I had attended services there and listened to the sermons, all of which had fortified my soul during the difficult years of persecution. Even almost six years of Nazi rule had not prepared me for such an experience.*

Aufbau, No. 26, December 1998, from HaGalil.com

After Hitler gained power, Jewish people left Germany if they could. However, the U.S. and European countries were still suffering from economic depression and would not accept many immigrants. In 1939, attempting to pacify the Palestinians, the British also restricted Jewish immigration to Palestine.

After World War II broke out in 1939, Nazi Germany occupied much of Europe and imposed anti-Semitic laws on the defeated populations. Jews were forbidden to leave, and it became extraordinarily difficult for them to escape. Many Jews from German-occupied countries were deported to Poland and forced to do hard labor for the Nazis. International Jewish organizations, such as the Joint Distribution Committee, rescued German Jews and helped them reach safe countries.

The Holocaust In 1941, Germany invaded the Soviet Union and other eastern European countries. Special German troops called the *Einsatzgruppen* rounded up Jews and Communists and murdered them. Later that year, the Nazis started to build "death camps." Jews from Nazi-occupied countries were transported to

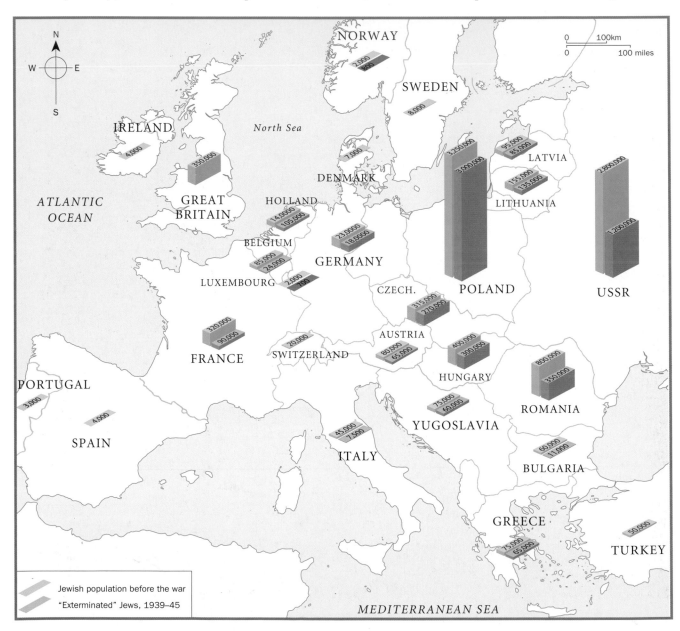

This map shows the Jewish populations of European countries before the start of World War II in 1939, and in 1945, after the Holocaust. The largest and oldest Jewish communities in the world were destroyed during the war.

these camps in cattle trucks and by train. The young and fit were forced to work, while the rest were killed—often in large groups—in gas chambers. It is estimated that between 1941 and 1945, six million Jews were brutally murdered, starved, beaten, or worked to death. This attempt to wipe out the entire Jewish population of Europe became known as the Holocaust.

Few nations helped the Jews, although some courageous individuals in European countries risked their own lives to save Jewish people from the Nazis. For instance, in 1943, the Nazis planned to deport the Jews of German-occupied Denmark to the death camps. Members of the Danish resistance movement helped many Jews to safety in Sweden, a country that was not involved in the war. Yet by the end of the war in 1945, about 70 percent of Europe's Jews had perished, and the Jewish culture of eastern Europe had been destroyed.

THE WARSAW GHETTO UPRISING

Despite the overwhelming power of the Nazis, Jewish people opposed them where they could. Some joined the Allied forces or the resistance effort; others resisted through armed revolt. The most significant revolt took place in the Warsaw Ghetto in Poland. The Nazis began deporting Jews from the ghetto to the death camps in July 1942. They deported two-thirds of the ghetto's 300,000 inhabitants. In January 1943, Nazi troops surrounded the ghetto, ready to send the remaining inhabitants to the death camps. Some of the inhabitants of the ghetto mounted a heroic defense, forcing the Nazis to fight the biggest battle on Polish soil since their occupation of Poland in 1939. The majority of those who participated in the revolt died while fighting, and the Nazis crushed the uprising in May 1943.

In April 1945, the Allied forces that had been fighting against Germany liberated the prisoners of the Buchenwald concentration camp. Most of the survivors were painfully thin and extremely ill. Only a minority of European Jews escaped the Nazis' efforts to annihilate an entire people.

After the war ended in 1945, most of the Jewish survivors in Europe were homeless. Some tried to return home to rebuild their lives, but the majority had nowhere to go and found themselves in Displaced Persons' (DP) camps in Germany and Austria. A minority was permitted to emigrate to the U.S. But in 1947, there were still 300,000 Jews in DP camps.

As the horrors of the Holocaust were revealed, there was worldwide sympathy for the Jewish people, giving fresh impetus to the Zionist movement. Around 69,000 homeless Jews attempted to go to Palestine, although it was illegal for large numbers to enter the country. The British government could no longer cope with the tensions between the Palestinians and Jews, so in 1947, the British announced their desire to end their mandate—control of Palestine—by May 1948. The United Nations (UN) was called upon to try to solve the conflict between the Jews and the Palestinians.

DAVID BEN-GURION (1886–1973)

As a young man in Poland, David Ben-Gurion was a committed Zionist, and he emigrated to Palestine at the age of 20. When World War I broke out, Ben-Gurion was expelled from Palestine (then ruled by the Ottoman Empire) for his Zionist activities. He returned to the country when the British took control. In 1920, Ben-Gurion founded the Histadrut, the Jewish workers' trade union, and the Israeli Workers' Party in 1930. In 1935, he was elected chairman of the Zionist Executive, which oversaw the Zionist movement. When the UK restricted immigration to Palestine in 1939, Ben-Gurion called on the Zionists to fight the British and make Palestine impossible to govern, in order to achieve a Jewish state. In May 1948, Ben-Gurion became the first prime minister of Israel.

David Ben-Gurion reads the Declaration of Independence at the Tel Aviv Museum; above him is a portrait of Theodor Herzl. The U.S. was the first country to recognize Israel.

The state of Israel The UN voted to divide Palestine between the Jews and the Palestinians, but the Palestinians did not agree to the partition plan. Fighting broke out between the Jews and the Palestinians. In May 1948, the state of Israel was declared a sovereign nation. The day after the declaration, the armies of Egypt, Jordan, Iraq, Syria, and Lebanon invaded Israel, starting a war that continued until January 1949. Under the final armistice agreement of July 1949, Israel secured over 77 percent of what was formerly Palestine—22 percent more territory than it had been offered under the UN plan. Jordan took over East Jerusalem and the West Bank, and Egypt occupied the Gaza Strip. Thus, the state of Israel did not include the entire area of the ancient land of Israel. It did include the holy cities of Safed—where four ancient synagogues survived—Tiberias, and the western part of Jerusalem. However, the Palestinians did not receive any territory, and approximately 726,000 people were forced to flee their country as refugees.

Between 1948 and 1951, the population of Israel expanded rapidly with the arrival of around 688,000 immigrants. Several thousand arrived from the DP camps of Europe. Jews came from Muslim countries, where sympathy with the Palestinians had led to anti-Israeli sentiment, and Jews no longer felt secure. Absorbing the immigrants was a huge challenge for the new state. Support came from the U.S., donations from the Diaspora, and reparations (compensation for war crimes) paid by Germany.

Legend:
- Jewish territory on the eve of independence
- Territory acquired by Israel 1948–49
- Armistice line 1949
- Arab countries

LEBANON

Tyre

Motullah

SYRIA

Acre

Safed

Galilee

Haifa

Tiberias

Sea of Galilee

Nazareth

Jezreel Valley

Beth-Shean

Hadera

Janin

Netanya

Tul Karm

Nabulus

MEDITERRANEAN SEA

Qalqilya

Tel Aviv

Petach Tikva

Jaffa

WEST BANK

Lod

Ramla

Ramallah

Yavneh

Jericho

Ashdod

Jerusalem

Gaza

Dead Sea

Hebron

GAZA STRIP

Ruhamah

Tekumah

Beersheba

Sedom

Gevulot

Haluza

JORDAN (formerly Transjordan)

EGYPT

Negev Desert

N
W E
S

Eilat

0   50km
0   50 miles

This map shows the territory gained by Israel during the war of 1948–49 and the borders defined by the armistice agreements of 1949.

CHAPTER 6:
JUDAISM IN THE POSTWAR WORLD

The new Jewish homeland did not enjoy peace. There was continual tension between Israel and its Arab neighbors. The Arab nations did not accept the Jewish state, and Israel was determined to defend itself against them. Meanwhile, up to 460,000 Palestinians remained in refugee camps in the West Bank and Gaza Strip, desperate to return to their homes within Israel.

Israeli soldiers after the capture of the Western Wall in East Jerusalem during the 1967 Arab-Israeli war. The Palestinians hope that East Jerusalem could be the capital of a future Palestinian state, yet Israel is unwilling to give up any part of Jerusalem.

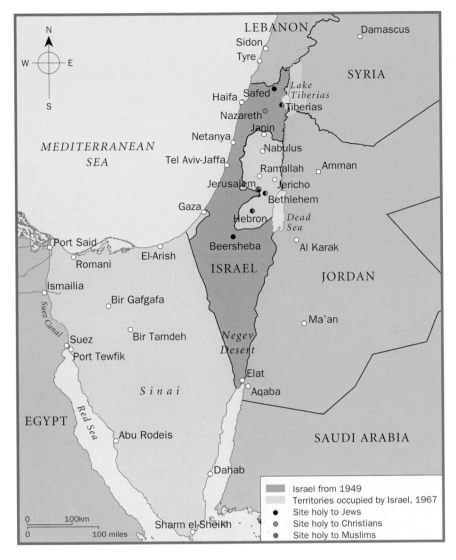

This map shows the territory gained by Israel in the 1967 war as well as holy sites in the country.

Map legend:
- Israel from 1949
- Territories occupied by Israel, 1967
- ● Site holy to Jews
- ● Site holy to Christians
- ● Site holy to Muslims

Israel expands

During the Arab-Israeli War of 1967, Israel conquered East Jerusalem, the West Bank, and the Gaza Strip and brought them under military occupation. The Jewish state now ruled a large part of historic Israel, including significant Jewish holy sites such as the holy city of Hebron and the Western Wall in Jerusalem. The Western Wall was the only part of the Second Temple in Jerusalem that remained after the Temple was destroyed in 70 CE. Throughout history, Jews have expressed grief at the destruction of the Temple and have wanted it to be restored. The site of the Temple is called the Temple Mount. It also includes significant Muslim holy sites—the Dome of the Rock and the Al-Aqsa Mosque. Since Israel took control of the area in 1967, there have been disputes with Palestinian Muslims over control and access to the Temple Mount.

There were other wars between Israel and the neighboring Arab countries in 1973 and 1982, as well as Palestinian uprisings against Israeli occupation from 1987 to 1993 and from 2000 to 2005. Since the 1970s, there have also been efforts to reach a peaceful settlement: Israel signed a peace treaty with Egypt in 1979 and with Jordan in 1994. Yet the core conflict between Israel and the Palestinians over territory and how to share it remains unresolved.

JEWS IN THE SOVIET UNION

The Soviet Union, also known as the USSR, was a country formed out of the territories of the Russian Empire following the Russian Revolution of 1917. In the Soviet Union, religious practice was discouraged, and quotas restricted the number of Jews allowed to go to college and obtain a profession. Jewish history and religious studies had to be taught in secret. Like all citizens of the Soviet Union, Jews were not permitted to leave the country, although after 1968, the rules were gradually relaxed, and Jews were allowed to emigrate to Israel. About 300,000 Jews left between 1969 and 1989. However, many did not want to live in Israel, and they subsequently made their way to the U.S. Following the fall of the Soviet Union in 1990, around one million Soviet Jews emigrated to Israel.

These Sephardi Jews from Morocco are at a festival to honor the Jewish philosopher Maimonides. The Sephardi and Ashkenazi communities in Israel each have their own chief rabbi to lead them.

The conflict is essentially a political problem with religious dimensions. While the majority of Israeli citizens is Jewish, the majority of the population of the West Bank and Gaza Strip is Muslim. How can Israel retain its Jewish nature if a large part of the population under its rule is non-Jewish? Of the population under Israel's control, there are 3.9 million mostly Muslim Palestinians in the West Bank and Gaza Strip and 1.3 million non-Jews (mostly Palestinians) within Israel. There are about 5.1 million Jews in Israel and the lands under its control. Israel is trying to address this issue by disengaging from areas where Palestinians are in the majority; it removed its armed forces and settlers from Gaza in 2005, while retaining overall military control. Yet owing to the higher birth rate of Muslim

Palestinians compared to Jews, many Israelis are concerned that Palestinians could become the majority in the state of Israel within 30 or 40 years.

On the other hand, how can Israel be truly democratic while the Palestinians in the West Bank and Gaza Strip remain under the military control of Israel and do not have the same rights as Israelis? Even Palestinians within Israel, although they are citizens of the state, suffer from discrimination in many areas of life.

Judaism in Israel Jews make up around four-fifths of Israel's population—the majority of the other one-fifth is Muslim Palestinian. The main groups of Jews are Ashkenazim from central and eastern Europe

RELIGIOUS LAWS IN ISRAEL

Religion affects how Israel is governed. For example:

● Kosher food is provided in the army and all government institutions.

● It is illegal to import nonkosher foods. However, although pork is not kosher, there are some Israeli pork farms; this meat is particularly popular among Russian immigrants.

● Jewish law governs marriage and divorce—it is not possible to have a civil (nonreligious) wedding.

● Most businesses close on the Jewish Sabbath (Saturday), and there is no public transportation on that day.

● The Law of Return (passed in 1950) allows any Jew from around the world to emigrate to Israel.

This map indicates the complex division of control between Israel and the Palestinians in 2006. Gaza was under Palestinian rule while Israel still occupied the West Bank. A security wall built on the West Bank divided the Palestinian territory from Israel.

and Sephardim from the Mediterranean region and North Africa. There are also Jews from western Europe, central Asia, and North and South America.

Jews in Israel tend to define themselves as either religious or nonreligious, rather than identifying themselves with a specific denomination, or branch of a religion. However, denominations do exist within Judaism (see pages 40–41). Among the nonreligious are people who call themselves secular Jews—they are mostly Ashkenazim. Others, mainly Sephardim, call themselves traditionalists. They are committed to Judaism but do not carry out all of the religious rituals. Nonreligious Jews do take part in some Jewish customs, to varying degrees. For example, most attend a seder at Passover. Many Israeli Jews feel they are expressing their Judaism simply by living in Israel, and they do not need to carry out religious rituals as well.

Those who describe themselves as religious are Orthodox, a term that covers a wide spectrum of religious practice. The most Orthodox are called Haredi Jews. They follow the traditions established in the written Torah and the Talmud, the earliest written form of the Halacha. They adopt an extremely modest dress code and live in their own separate community.

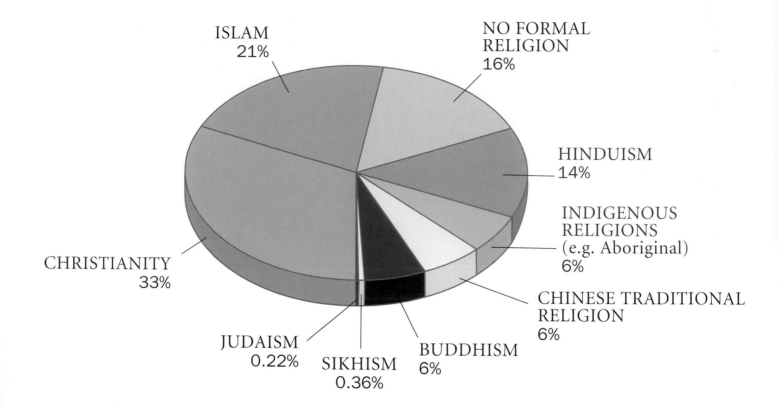

A pie chart showing the number of Jewish people compared to other world faiths.

Judaism in the Diaspora Within the Diaspora, there is a wide variety of religious practice. Many Jews are secular or completely assimilated into their country's culture.

Movements within modern Judaism range from the most Orthodox, to the Conservative and Reform movements, to the Reconstructionists. The term Orthodox covers all those who strictly observe the traditional practices of Judaism.

Founded in the U.S. in the early twentieth century, the Conservative movement is based on the belief that the truths of the Jewish scriptures come from God but were transmitted by humans. Conservative Jews accept the Halacha but believe that it should be flexible and adapt to social changes, while also staying true to Jewish values. The movement is committed to supporting Israel; many Conservative Jews feel that Jewish nationalism is a vital part of their culture. In Israel, the Conservative branch of Judaism is called the Masorti movement.

Reform Judaism is the largest Jewish movement in the United States. Reform Jews accept that all Jewish people should study their traditions and carry out the mitzvoth that are relevant to modern society. They believe that their religion has evolved over time and will continue to do so. Each individual has the right to decide whether to adopt a particular belief or practice. Reform Jews believe in equality and are committed to social justice.

Another form of Judaism is the Reconstructionist movement, founded in the U.S. in 1922. This group believes that Judaism is a culture that was developed by human beings. They do not believe that the Torah is the word of God, rather that Jewish people should maintain their culture and identity by carrying out religious rituals and learning their history. Reconstructionists also believe that they should mix freely with other people and work to promote values of freedom and justice. Like Conservative Jews, Reconstructionists support Israel as the Jewish homeland.

THE MESSIAH

There is a traditional Jewish belief that one day the Messiah will come, a man who will rebuild the Temple in Jerusalem, gather all of the Jews to Israel, and unite all people in the knowledge of the God of Israel. He will end all hatred, disease, and suffering and bring world peace: *Nation shall not lift up sword against nation, neither shall man learn war anymore.*

Isaiah 2:4

Jewish families keep their traditions alive at the seder meal by retelling the story of the Jews' escape from Egypt.

The future Some people believe that the future of Judaism is bleak. The religious community is split. Orthodox Jews do not accept the other traditions as valid, while most Reform and Conservative Jews do not believe that the Torah is God's word. The number of Jews worldwide is declining, and many marry non-Jews and assimilate into mainstream society. Eventually, Jewish traditions may disappear.

Others argue that Judaism has always adapted to new situations. Although religious observance is declining, sufficient numbers will remain faithful to the Torah and the synagogue. Many secular Jews retain their Jewish identity and links with the community. Although Judaism is fragmented, it will nevertheless survive as a major world faith.

GREAT LIVES

Moses Maimonides (1135–1204)

Born in Córdoba, Spain, Maimonides's family was forced to practice Judaism in secret after the Islamic dynasty, the Almohads, captured the city in 1148. Maimonides had a traditional Jewish education but also studied scientific subjects. Beginning in 1159, his family moved several times to avoid religious persecution, eventually settling in al-Fustat, Egypt. Maimonides became the court physician to the military leader Saladin, while also acting as a leading member of the Jewish community and writing numerous works. His most important were the Mishneh Torah (1178), a code of Jewish law, and *The Guide of the Perplexed* (1191), in which he argued that there is no contradiction between reason and faith because both come from God.

Israel ben Eliezer (ca. 1700–60)

It is thought that Israel ben Eliezer (also known as the Ba'al Shem Tov, or the Besht) was born in the village of Okup in the Carpathian Mountains, in eastern Europe. He made a living as a religious slaughterer—killing animals for meat according to the kosher food laws. Beginning in 1736, he devoted himself to spiritual pursuits and founded a movement that became known as Hasidism. Hasidism was a popular movement, and the Besht held discussions with ordinary people as well as rabbis. He believed that every human action, carried out with God in mind, was equal to following the commandments. The Besht believed people should worship joyfully and encouraged singing, dancing, and storytelling. The Hasidic movement spread throughout eastern Europe after ben Eliezer's death.

Elijah ben Solomon Zalman, the "Vilna Gaon" (1720–97)

Between 1740 and 1745, Zalman traveled among the Jewish communities of Poland and Germany before settling in Vilna, Lithuania, the cultural center of eastern European Jewish life. A distinguished scholar of Jewish literature, he was given the title gaon (excellency). He

wrote many commentaries on Jewish scripture. Zalman led the opposition to Hasidism and temporarily checked the spread of the movement in Lithuania.

Moses Mendelssohn (1729–86)

Born in Dessau, Germany, in 1743, Moses Mendelssohn moved to Berlin as a child. In 1754, he joined the business of silk manufacturer Issak Bernhard. By working alongside non-Jews and holding discussions with them, Mendelssohn showed that Jews could be included in mainstream culture while maintaining their traditions. He was one of the leaders of the Haskalah, the Jewish Enlightenment. Mendelssohn tried to combine Judaism with the ideas of the European Enlightenment, such as the belief that the universe could be explained rationally without referring to God. His efforts helped lay the foundations for the Reform movement.

Samson Raphael Hirsch (1808–88)

Born in Hamburg, Germany, Hirsch became the chief rabbi of Oldenburg in 1830. He adopted Reformist habits, such as delivering sermons in German, and he thought Jews should be involved in modern Western culture. However, he had traditional religious views. He held that the Torah came from God and that the laws could not be changed in the light of historical developments. In 1836, he published a defense of traditional Judaism entitled the *Nineteen Letters on Judaism*. He decided that traditional Jews, who became known as Orthodox Jews, should organize separately from Reform Jews.

Theodor Herzl (1860–1904)

Herzl was born in Budapest, Hungary, but his family moved to Vienna in 1878. He studied at the University of Vienna, where he experienced anti-Semitism. After completing his studies, Herzl became a writer, playwright, and journalist. Following the Dreyfus Affair in 1894, when Jewish officer Captain Albert Dreyfus was unjustly accused of treason (the crime of betraying one's country), Herzl concluded that anti-Semitism would always exist. He published *The Jewish State* in 1896, in which he argued that the Jewish people needed their own homeland. At the first Zionist Congress in Switzerland in 1897, the World Zionist Organization was founded to work toward such a state. Herzl's goal was achieved within 50 years of his death.

Golda Meir (1898–1978)

Golda Meir was born in Kiev in Ukraine. Her family moved to the U.S. in 1906 to escape poverty. Meir joined a Zionist group in high school, and in 1921, she emigrated to Palestine. In 1924, she became an official of the Histadrut trade union. After World War II, she raised funds in the U.S. to help cover the costs of the Zionists' war with the Arabs. Following the establishment of Israel, Meir held various roles in government, and in 1971, she became prime minister. In 1973, Israel was invaded by Egypt and Syria, sparking the Yom Kippur War; Meir's government was blamed for failing to anticipate the attack, and she resigned in 1974.

FURTHER INFORMATION

Books

DK Eyewitness Guides: Judaism by Douglas Charing (Dorling Kindersley, 2003)

Exploring Religions: Judaism by Anne Geldart (Heinemann Library, 2001)

Great Religious Leaders: Moses and Judaism by Sharon Barron (Hodder Wayland, 2005)

Religion in Focus: Judaism by Geoff Teece (Franklin Watts Ltd, 2003)

Religions Today: Judaism Today by Cavan Wood (Heinemann Library, 2003)

World Religions: Judaism by Ian Graham (Walrus Books, 2005)

Books for older readers and resources for teachers

A Historical Atlas of the Jewish People by Eli Barnavi (Schocken Books, 2003)

The Student's Encyclopedia of Judaism by Geoffrey Wigoder and Fred Skolnick (New York University Press, 2004)

Web sites

http://judaism.about.com/
A Web site all about Jewish practices, beliefs, and culture.

http://www.torah.org/
A Web site covering the basics and features of Jewish law and ethics.

www.jewishvirtuallibrary.org/jsource/index.html
The Jewish Virtual Library. There are links to information about Jewish history and religion, Jewish women, the state of Israel, and other topics. The site is run by the American-Israeli Cooperative Enterprise.

FACTS AND FIGURES

Calendar of Festivals and Holy Days

There are 12 lunar months in the Jewish calendar. In some years there is a "leap month" to keep festivals in their season. Orthodox Jews outside Israel celebrate some festivals for an extra day.

Month and number of days of festival	Event	What happens
September, 1–2 days	Rosh Hashanah: the Jewish New Year	The rabbi blows the shofar (ram's horn) to represent spiritual awakening. People eat apples and honey for a sweet new year.
September/October, 1 day	Yom Kippur	People fast for 25 hours and confess their wrongdoings to God.
September/October, 7–8 days	Sukkoth	People live in huts called sukkoth (singular: sukkah) to remember when the Jews lived in temporary shelters during their journey from Egypt to Canaan.
September/October, 1–2 days	Simhath Torah	People show their love for the Torah; they parade the Torah scrolls in the synagogue and in the streets.
December, 8 days	Hanukkah	People light candles and eat food cooked in oil to remember how the Maccabees restored the Temple.
January, 1 day	Tu B'Shvat	Jews in Israel plant trees (New Year for Trees). Outside Israel, Jewish people taste 15 fruits to show the importance of caring for the environment.
February/March, 1 day	Purim	People dress up and listen to the biblical story of Esther, who risked her life to save the Jewish people.
March/April, 7–8 days	Passover	People gather to tell the story of the Jews' escape from Egypt; during the festival, Jews eat flat crackers called matzos instead of bread.
June, 1–2 days	Shabuoth	This festival celebrates God's gift of the Torah to Moses. People read the Torah and eat dairy foods.
August, 1 day	Tishah-b'Ab	People fast to remember the destruction of the Jewish Temple and other tragedies.

List of Holy sites

Beersheba (page 4)

Hebron (pages 5, 37)

Rachel's Tomb, near Bethlehem (page 5)

Safed (pages 14, 21, 35)

Temple Mount, Jerusalem (page 37)

Tiberias (pages 10, 35)

The Tomb of the Patriarchs, Abraham, Isaac, Jacob, and their wives, near the Western Wall, Jerusalem (page 5)

The world's Jewish population (2005)

Africa	226,000
Asia	5,327,000
Europe	2,015,000
North America	6,179,000
Oceania	105,000
South America	1,221,000
Total	**15,073,000**

Source: Encyclopedia Britannica, 2006

TIME LINE

ca. 1800 Abraham and his clan leave Ur in Mesopotamia and move to Canaan.

ca. 1000 The kingdom of Israel is established; Saul is the first king.

928 King Solomon dies. The northern Israelite tribes set up the kingdom of Israel; the southern tribes establish Judah.

722 The Assyrians capture Samaria and deport the Israelites.

586 The Babylonians conquer Jerusalem and destroy the Temple; they defeat the Kingdom of Judah.

538 King Cyrus the Great of Persia conquers Babylon and allows exiles in Babylon to return to their homeland.

332 King Alexander of Macedonia conquers Judah.

164 Judah Maccabee leads a Jewish rebellion and recaptures Jerusalem.

63 The Romans conquer the lands of Israel and Syria.

CE

ca. 28–30 Jesus is a teacher and healer in Palestine, and Christianity begins.

70 The Romans conquer Jerusalem and destroy the Second Temple.

132 Simon Bar Kokhba leads a Jewish revolt and drives the Romans out of Jerusalem.

135 The Jews are defeated; most are dispersed to different lands.

1290 The Jews are expelled from England.

1394 The Jews are expelled from France.

1492 The Jews are driven out of Spain.

1648 The Cossacks rebel against the Polish nobility in the Khmelnytsky rebellion.

1897 The World Zionist Organization is founded.

1897 The Bund is established.

1917 The Balfour Declaration expresses British support for a Jewish homeland in Palestine.

1920 The British Mandate (rule over territory of the former Ottoman Empire) is established in Palestine.

1933 Adolf Hitler is appointed chancellor of Germany.

1936–39 Palestinian rebellion against Jewish immigration to Palestine.

1938 During Kristallnacht, Jewish property is destroyed all over Germany and Austria.

1939 World War II breaks out.

1943 The Warsaw Ghetto Uprising against the Nazis.

1945 World War II ends.

1948 The state of Israel is established.

1948–49 War between Israel and the Arab states.

1956 The Suez War: Israel, France, and the UK go to war with Egypt over control of the Suez Canal.

1967 The Six-Day War between Israel and the Arabs.

1979 Israel signs a peace treaty with Egypt.

1984 An Israeli rescue operation brings the Ethiopian Jews to Israel.

1987–93 Palestinian intifada (uprising) against Israeli rule.

1990 The fall of the USSR allows large numbers of Jews to emigrate.

1994 Israel signs a peace treaty with Jordan.

2000–05 Second Palestinian intifada against Israeli occupation.

GLOSSARY

anti-Semitism Hostility toward the Jewish people.

Ashkenazi Means "Germany" in Hebrew; it refers to Jews of eastern European origin.

assimilation Becoming a part of the majority culture in a society and losing Jewish identity.

Black Death A serious infectious disease, also known as The Plague, that struck Europe from 1347 to 1351, killing an estimated one-third of the population.

Bund The General Union of Jewish Workers in Lithuania, Poland, and Russia. A socialist and non-Zionist party that was founded in Vilna, Lithuania, in 1897.

circumcision A Jewish custom that involves cutting off the foreskin of the penis of a baby boy to show that he is a member of the Jewish community.

Conservative Judaism A modern, non-Orthodox branch of Judaism that maintains elements of traditional Judaism while allowing for some modernization of religious practices.

converso A Spanish Jew who converted to Christianity in the late fourteenth and fifteenth centuries.

death camps Camps set up by the Nazis during World War II where millions of people, mostly Jews, were killed or worked to death.

Diaspora The Jewish communities living outside Palestine or, since 1948, outside Israel.

Einsatzgruppen During World War II, Nazi units entered Soviet territories and murdered Jews, Communists, and Romanies (traveling people).

ethnic group A group of people bound together by a common culture, tradition, and sometimes language.

exodus A mass departure. The second book of the Torah, the book of Exodus, includes a description of the exodus of the Israelites from Egypt.

gaon A Hebrew word meaning "excellence." Gaon was the title given to the head of a yeshiva in third-century Babylonia and later to respected scholars of the Talmud.

ghetto Beginning in the fourteenth century, a part of a city where Jews were forced to live. Ghettos were established in some Muslim countries and throughout Europe.

guild An association of craftsmen or merchants formed for mutual aid and protection and to further their interests.

Hagaddah Meaning "telling," the book read and discussed during the seder meal at Passover.

Halacha Jewish law that, according to tradition, is based on the original law given to Moses by God. The Halacha is the totality of laws that have evolved since biblical times to regulate religious and daily life.

Haredi Judaism The most Orthodox form of Judaism; Haredi Jews believe their beliefs and religious practices date back to the Torah as it was received by Moses.

Hasidic movement From *hasidut*, meaning "piety." The movement, founded by the Ba'al Shem Tov in eighteenth-century eastern Europe, focused on spirituality and joy in worship.

Haskalah From the Hebrew word for "common sense," the Haskalah was the Jewish Enlightenment, a movement among European Jews in the late eighteenth century. Its followers believed in studying secular as well as Jewish studies in order to fit in better within European society.

Histadrut A Jewish trade union, established in Palestine in 1920 to help Jewish workers find jobs and provide benefits such as sick pay.

Kabbala The tradition of Jewish mysticism that began in the twelfth century.

Karaism A movement within Judaism that began in eighth-century Persia and proclaimed the written Torah as the sole source of Jewish law.

kosher Food that is prepared according to Jewish law.

kuppah A collection box for donations to help the poorest members of the Jewish community.

Ladino The language spoken by Sephardi Jews and used in their literature. Including medieval Spanish as well as Hebrew words, it is written using the Hebrew alphabet.

maskilim The followers of the Haskalah, the Jewish Enlightenment.

Mishna The oldest collection of Jewish laws, compiled by numerous scholars and put into its final form by Judah ha-Nasi in the third century CE.

Mishneh Torah An extensive commentary on the Talmud, written by Jewish scholar Moses Maimonides in the twelfth century.

Mitnaggedim (singular: Mitnagged) The opponents of the Hasidic movement in eastern Europe.

mitzvoth (singular: mitzvah) A commandment; also, a charitable deed.

neo-Orthodox The movement established by Samson Raphael Hirsch in the nineteenth century that believed Jewish people should follow traditional practices but could also have a secular education.

Orthodox Used to describe Jews who follow traditional practices, the term arose in the nineteenth century to distinguish traditional Jews from Reform Jews.

Passover The festival at which Jewish people remember the Jews' escape from slavery in Egypt.

pogrom An organized massacre of a group of people; the term is used to refer to the attacks on Jewish communities in eastern Europe in the late nineteenth and early twentieth centuries.

quota A fixed number of people from a particular group who are allowed to enter a country each year.

rabbi In ancient times, a scholar who explained the written and oral Torah. From the Middle Ages, the term came to mean the spiritual leader of a particular Jewish community.

Reconstructionism A movement founded in the U.S. in 1922 that holds that Judaism is a religious culture but does not accept that the Torah is the word of God.

Reform Judaism A movement that has reformed many traditional beliefs, laws, and practices in an effort to adapt Judaism to the modern world.

Resistance Fighters who were not part of an official army and who operated behind enemy lines during World War II, attacking the Nazis and their allies.

ritual purity Maintaining the laws of ritual cleansing; Jews immerse themselves in a bath called a mikvah to make themselves ritually pure—for example, before a festival.

Sanhedrin An assembly of scholars that acted as the supreme religious and legal body of the Jewish community in Palestine during the Roman period.

seder The Passover meal at which the story of the exodus from Egypt is read.

Sephardi Meaning "Spain" in Hebrew, it refers to descendants of the Spanish and Portuguese Jews who were expelled from their countries at the end of the fifteenth century.

Shabbat The Jewish Sabbath, which lasts from sunset on Friday until sunset on Saturday.

shtetl A Yiddish word meaning a Jewish village in eastern Europe.

Shulchan Arukh A sixteenth-century compilation of Jewish law and practice that is still the basis for Orthodox religious observance.

socialist Believing in a system in which there is no private property and there is collective ownership of the means of production, including factories and other things used to produce goods.

synagogue The Jewish house of worship and the place where Jews gather for community events and study.

Talmud A record of the oral law. There were two versions: one compiled in Palestine in the fifth century CE and one compiled in Babylonia in the sixth century CE. The Babylonian version is widely accepted as more authoritative.

Torah The first five books of the Bible: Genesis, Exodus, Leviticus, Numbers, and Deuteronomy.

yeshiva (plural: yeshivas) An academy for studying the Talmud.

Yiddish The language of Ashkenazi Jews, which is similar to German. It incorporates Hebrew words and is written using the Hebrew alphabet.

zaddik (plural: zaddikim) In the Hasidic movement, a Jewish spiritual leader who was seen as a mediator between people and God.

Zionism The movement founded in the late nineteenth century to promote the establishment of a homeland for the Jewish people in Palestine.

INDEX

DATE DUE

HIGHSMITH 45230